PROMISES DON'T DIE

The Legacy Lives Series

Bishop Andrew Merritt

The Legacy Lives Series
Promises Don't Die
©2018 Bishop Andrew Merritt

Book Cover Design by ADEI Media Group (adeimedia.com)

Unless otherwise indicated, all Scripture quotations are taken from the King James Version of the Holy Bible.

"Scripture taken from the New King James Version®. Copyright © 1982 by Thomas Nelson. Used by permission. All rights reserved."

"Scripture taken from the NEW AMERICAN STANDARD BIBLE®, Copyright 1960, 1962, 1963, 1971, 1972, 1973, 1977, 1995 by The Lockman Foundation. Used by permission."

"Scripture quotations taken from the Amplified® Bible (AMP), Copyright © 2015 by the Lockman Foundation. Used by permission." (www.Lockman.org)

ISBN-13: 978-0-9637640-9-6

Bishop Andrew Merritt Ministries
www.bishopmerrittministries.org

All rights reserved.
No part of this book may be reproduced in any manner whatsoever, without written permission from Bishop Andrew Merritt Ministries.

Printed in the United States of America.

"But Abram said, 'Lord God, what will You give me, seeing I go childless…?"
(Genesis 15:2 NKJV)

Everyone has been given a promise from God. Some have been long forgotten, left in a heap of disappointment in your heart too painful to touch. Time soured the expectation that some things will ever come to pass. As the seasons changed and life leathered your skin, the wind was sure to whisper, "Don't you dare believe that again." So as quick as a scolded child, you snatched your faith back, retreated to a place of unbelief, adjusting yourself back to the status quo.

Recently, I thought about the loss of a woman who birthed more than ten children at my church. I was chatting with someone about how one of her children seemed to be going astray. I listened and prayed. Then the Holy Spirit reminded me that this mother believed for her children, even up to the day she transitioned from this life.

Some of them are more committed to God than others at the time I write this book. But her face became ever present reminding me that 'Promises Don't Die.' Yes, she is no longer in the earth, but the promises over her children remain here. Who said that the promises leave when we do?

The Promise Is Not About You

"Declaring the end from the beginning, and from ancient times things which have not been done, saying, 'My purpose will be established, and I will accomplish all My good pleasure.'" (Isaiah 46:10 NASB)

When Abram asked the Lord what he was going to give him, seeing that he was without an heir, God was gracious to answer him. But if you look at the response to his question, God focused on His purpose more than He did to Abram's desire.

"And behold the word of the Lord came unto him, saying, "This shall not be thine heir; but he that shall come forth out of thine own bowels shall be thine heir.' And he brought him fort abroad, and said, 'Look now toward heaven, and tell the stars, if thou be able to number them:' and he said unto him, 'So shall thy seed be.' And he believed in the Lord and he counted it to him for righteousness." (Genesis 15:4-6)

Of course, it was good news for Abram to hear God reaffirm that he was going to experience the joy of having an heir, not just an heir—a son. You see God had called Abram to start a new line, a lineage of descendants that His Son was going to come through. Isaac was going to bring joy to Abram's heart. But Jesus was going to bring joy to the Father's.

When God called Abram, he brought Lot with him. A direct disobedient act that would need to be rectified, one way or another. I believe he'd brought Lot with him as a crutch. God told him not only to leave his father's house, but his kindred (family members) as well. But Abram brought Lot anyway. I believe Lot was Abram's 'just in case', but God wasn't having that.

See, the promise comes with two sides. One side is *life* and the other is *death*. The life of God is in His spoken Word to you. It's the breath of God, the same one that is circulating in your lungs right now keeps a promise alive.

God had already spoken, which meant that wild horses couldn't have caused Lot to stay with Abram. I know Abram was heartbroken. He fought for Lot at every turn. But God wanted a new line and you can't put new wine in old skins, (Matthew 9:17). Lot was a remnant from his idol worshipping Dad's lineage. He couldn't use Lot to slip Himself into, even if He wanted to.

Lot displayed rebellion against Abram and ultimately God at every turn. *"For rebellion is as the sin of witchcraft, and stubbornness is as iniquity and idolatry. Because you have rejected the word of the Lord, He has also rejected you from being king,"* (1 Samuel 15:23 NKJV). The heart of idolatry was still in Lot, which meant that he had disqualified himself from partaking in the blessing that God was setting in place for all of mankind.

Sarai was barren, and Abram didn't have a son, so I'm sure he planned for Lot to be his surrogate heir. But God doesn't make surrogate promises—He doesn't need to since He is life itself.

When Lot walked away, Abram's crutch was gone, and I believe Genesis 15:2 was his defining moment. He wanted an heir and he needed a son.

I can tell you first hand what that means to a man. My eldest son, Jonathan had been my, *"So shall thy seed be,"* moment. It was a turning point of my faith in God. I didn't have a crutch. There was no nephew. And I knew that my lovely daughters were going to leave home one day to carry on the name of another man's house.

I had to believe for a son, there was no way around it. I had to straighten my back, grab my heart in hand, and stand there on what would seem to be the most ludicrous thing in the world—a promise from God.

Abram had come to the same moment of decision. He knew, like I did that there was nothing else to grab on to catch his balance in case things didn't go like he planned. There was only one Word from God, *"I am thy shield and thy exceeding great reward...but he that shall come forth out of thine own bowels shall be thine heir."*

There was nothing left, except to take a deep breath, steady yourself, and stand on the promise of God. So, I did.

When my wife conceived my son, my feet were so planted in the promise of God to me, I boldly declared, "My wife is carrying my son and by the way, he's going to be born on my birthday!" I can't say that I can remember any person that believed my enthusiastic declaration other than my wife. I thank God for her stand of faith, because when I look back, Abram didn't even have that.

I'm sure Sarai was a wonderful woman, but I believe Sarai represents many of you today. She had waited to the point of wither. Meaning her faith withered with the wind as each season passed her by. It hurt too much to believe. She had watched her body change. Her menstrual cycle had stopped (Genesis 18:11). Her womb was a tomb as far as she was concerned, and not only did she lack a direct visitation from God, she didn't have a promise to call her own.

But there is good news!

We know today what Sarai didn't. She would be the first demonstration of what God can do with dead things. Jesus was placed in the "heart of the earth." His resurrection from the dead would shake hell to it's knees and it would start with her silent womb and a promise from God to her one day.

"And he said, 'I will certainly return unto thee according to the time of life; and lo, Sarah thy wife shall have a son. And Sarah heard it in the tent door, which was behind him." (Genesis 18:10 NKJV)

The moment God speaks to your situation, everything starts moving to bring that spoken Word to pass!

"So will MY word be which goes forth from My mouth; it will not return to Me empty, without accomplishing what I desire, and without succeeding in the matter for which I sent it." (Isaiah 55:11 NASB)

Start looking at your promise as a life. Listen, the Word of God is the life of God!

Think of it this way. Once God speaks a promise to you, birth happens—a life is formed. That life (promise) is created to complete the task of accomplishing whatever it was created for. Your promise only answers to God Himself. It doesn't answer to you. It doesn't get its direction from you and I have even better news...it's not dependent on you!

Hallelujah!

When God spoke my son to me, the promise was birthed in my wife. And that promise was not going to go return back to God saying, "Hey, sorry God. I hate to tell you, I'm empty handed. I couldn't accomplish that because your son, Andrew and daughter, Viveca wouldn't get on board with me."

No! It will not return to God empty and unfulfilled. Do you know what that means? When we believed God for my son, Jonathan, the promise was already at work accomplishing the Word. All we did was attach our faith to a working Word! The promise was sent to succeed, because there is no failure in God.

There are many of you who have a promise from God that has been spoken to you but you have given up on it. But it's time to at least bring the promise a glass of water. Hydrate your faith! Stand up and coach the promise of God to success in your life. It's working, but you need to be the promise's cheerleader.

Speak the promise of God to you out of your mouth. I did. I realized that the promise was at work and my words could give strength to the promise bringing God back a successful outcome. The spoken Word is not dependent on you to live. However, the ability for that Word to return to God accomplished does.

"And he [Abram] believed in the Lord and he counted it to him for righteousness." (Genesis 15:6 NKJV)

"So from one man, though he was [physically] as good as dead, were born as many descendants as the stars of heaven in number, and innumerable as the same on the seashore." (Hebrews 11:12 AMP)

Abraham is not here! But the promise is STILL accomplishing what God desires and succeeding in the matter for which it was sent.

My son, is one of the pastors of our church. The Word that went forth out of God's mouth is STILL accomplishing what God desires and succeeding in the matter for which it was sent.

Even when God told Abraham to take Isaac to Mount Moriah to sacrifice his son, his only son, Abraham walked up that mountain, knife, rope and promise in tow. He knew that the promise still had some accomplishing to do and some succeeding to manifest.

How do I know this? Because Isaac was one star and God had promised Abram more stars than he could count.

Recently, I received a call that my son, Jonathan had died. Hearing those words felt as though someone had sucked the breath out of my body in an instant. For a minute, I can't tell you how I was able to breath. But I believe the promise of God, the very life of God expanded and contracted my lungs that day, giving me spiritual CPR.

By the time I heard my son's voice, God had reminded me that Jonathan was only one star, but He had promised me many. So, when an unexpected accident that threatened the life of my son and his wife occurred, I looked up at the stars and remembered that God has a promise working to accomplish and it is determined to succeed.

Then I watched the promise to him go in overdrive, as he wrote his first book, *STEP Out! Leave Your Imprint on the World* detailing the events of the accident and his recovery as a tool to help others live out the promise of God to them in their lives.

Promise Partners

"Then said the Lord unto me, "Thou hast well seen: for I will hasten [watch over] my word to perform it." (Jeremiah 1:12)

Remember that the promise of God is a *working* Word that He has sent forth to accomplish or perform a task or set of tasks in your life.

As believers in Jesus Christ, we have only one response to anything that He speaks, and that is "Yes," because His response is always, "Yes."

"For the Son of God, Jesus Christ, who was proclaimed among you by me and Silnaus and Timothy, was not 'Yes' and 'No,' but in Him it has always been 'Yes.'

For the promises of God are "Yes" in Christ. And so through Him, our 'Amen' is spoken to the glory of God." (2 Corinthians 1:20 NKJV)

Your agreement with God, partners you with the promise of God. No, the promise is not dependent on you, because as much as you benefit from the promise, you must always remember that it's God's purpose that is the object of any promise. Not yours.

We are given the awesome opportunity to be part of what God is doing in the earth. But even when you leave this earth, God's promise will still be at work accomplishing and succeeding; not on your behalf, but on His.

When you grab that truth, then you come to understand that the Word that you are running from is the very Word that you should be running towards. The wind that has whispered the lies of satan in your ear has no power to disengage your faith from the Word that the Lord God has spoken over you, you children, your family, your business, your ministry, and so on.

Stand up and grab the Word that God has spoken over your life in your heart. For some of you it may take a moment to locate because of all the past failures, hurts, disappointments, and unbelief. That's okay, I'll wait. Because we are going to change our posture, by standing upright in the power and authority of Almighty God.

No more crutches. No more, "What if it doesn't come to pass." No more excuses. No more unbelief. It's time to dig in and stand firm on God's Word to you. No wobbling when it looks hard. No crying when you don't see anything happening. No slouching when people call you, "Crazy." No, not this time.

Once you take the responsibility of the work of the Word off you, then obedience to the fellowship of the Spirit directs your steps and leads you in a plain path (Psalm 27:11). You become a partner in carrying a yoke that is easy and a burden that is light (Matthew 11:28-30). Partnering with the promise of God opens you up to see miracles, regardless of tribulation and triumph in spite of trials.

A Perpetual Promise
"And he brought him forth abroad, and said, 'Look now toward heaven, and tell the stars, if thou be able to number them: and he said unto him, so shall thy seed be.'" (Genesis 15:5)

To every believer in Jesus, **You** are *'thy seed be.'*

Jesus was the conduit for the promise to flow from one person to another. On the cross Jesus became the star gazer. When He couldn't see the Father, I believe He saw the stars. Those same stars that Abram saw that night gathered, as a reminder that there was a promise that had a perpetual (on-going, never-ending, never-changing) assignment. Descendants were at stake and He was the promise embodied.

There was no way He was going back to His Father empty-handed, without accomplishing what the Father desired and without succeeding in the matter for which He was sent.

He was THE Promise...and you become The Promise too when you receive Jesus as a drink offering of love from the Father. The promise God made to Abram is still at work, through wars and rumors of wars, famine and frustration, genocide and generations, the promise is still at work multiplying descendants through a blood sacrifice and an empty grave.

Promises don't die...they persevere through the ages. Because the life of a promise comes from the breath of God, not the performance of a person.

So, when Abram asked a question: *"What will you give me, seeing I go childless...?"*

God boldly, gave him an answer: *"I'm giving you...a promise."*

assignment. Descendants were at stake and He was the promise embodied.

There was no way He was going back to His Father empty-handed, without accomplishing what the Father desired and without succeeding in the matter for which He was sent.

He was THE Promise...and you become The Promise too when you receive Jesus as a drink offering of love from the Father. The promise God made to Abram is still at work, through wars and rumors of wars, famine and frustration, genocide and generations, the promise is still at work multiplying descendants through a blood sacrifice and an empty grave.

Promises don't die...they persevere through the ages. Because the life of a promise comes from the breath of God, not the performance of a person.

So, when Abram asked a question: *"What will you give me, seeing I go childless...?"*

God boldly, gave him an answer: *"I'm giving you...a promise."*

NY, a Master's Degree of Theology from New Covenant Theological Seminary in New York, and an Honorary Doctorate of Ministry from Logus Graduate School in Jacksonville, FL.

Bishop Andrew Merritt was elevated to the office of Bishop on November 24, 1990. His wife, Viveca C. Merritt, shares joint responsibility as Pastor of Straight Gate International Church. Bishop Merritt has six children: Anita, April, Rachelle (Lorne), Laura (Marc), Jonathan (Tatianna) and David. He is grandfather to Haki, Kirkland, Mariah, Lorne II, Aaron Andrew, Ryan, Lillian, Josiah, Cristina, and Andrew II.

www.ingramcontent.com/pod-product-compliance
Lightning Source LLC
Chambersburg PA
CBHW050609300426
44112CB00013B/2139